Weighed in the BALANCES

How Would Christ Evaluate Your Faith?

BENJAMIN H. WOODCOX

Copyright © 2019
By Benjamin H. Woodcox
All rights reserved. No part of this publication may be reproduced, stored in a retrieval system, or transmitted in any form or by any means—for example, electronic, photocopy, and recording—without the prior written permission of the publisher. The only exception is brief quotations in printed reviews.

Scripture taken from the New King James Version. Copyright © 1982 by Thomas Nelson, Inc. Used by permission. All rights reserved.

Editing Linda Stubblefield
Content Review Matthew Flenar
Cover Kelly Woodcox, design concept Linda Stubblefield

ISBN: 9781688292499 (Paperback Edition)

Contents

Preface	v
Introduction	vii
Ephesus— the Loveless Church	1
Smyrna— The Poor/Persecuted Church	13
Pergamos— The Compromising Church	25
Thyatira— The Corrupt Church	37
Sardis—The Dead Church	49
Philadelphia— The Faithful Church	59
Laodicea— The Lukewarm Church	69

Preface

James 4:14-15 declares...

"For what *is* your life? It is even a vapor that appears for a little time and then vanishes away... If the Lord wills, we shall live...."

Considering that we have a God who ultimately determines if we have another day on this earth is an awesome thought. My prayer is for many more to come to this realization and turn to Christ before it is too late and *for Christ to be the greatest treasure of all to those who call Him Lord!*

Introduction
Weighed in the Balances

The year was 539 BC, and Belshazzar, the reigning king of Babylon, was throwing a lavish party. The king's celebration was very bold and brazen—even rather careless in light of the great battle that ensued outside the city. The enemy army had surrounded the city, threatening to overtake them. Belshazzar obviously felt secure within the mighty city of Babylon with its 22-feet-thick and 90-feet-high walls[1]. The king of Babylon had yet to learn a truth that every person and nation should remember: God alone preserves men as well as nations, and God brings down men and cities—even those with formidable walls—if He so determines.

As foolish as the partying in a time of war was, of its own accord, the partying was not Belshazzar's biggest "fumble." Caught up in his party, and probably as a result of trying to impress others, Belshazzar issues orders to bring the vessels that had been removed from the Jewish Temple of Jerusalem (in the Babylonian destruction of the city, *c.* 587 BC) to use in their revelry. In so doing, Belshazzar openly mocked the one true God—committing sacrilege.

---

[1] Guzik, D. "Study Guide for Daniel 5 by David Guzik." Blue Letter Bible. Last Modified 21 Feb, 2017. https://www.blueletterbible.org/Comm/guzik_david/StudyGuide2017-Dan/Dan-5.cfm

In today's climate, people are casual about committing sacrilege when they should be concerned. *Sacrilege* is taking something that has been set aside for God and using it for other purposes. The results of Belshazzar's casual order were *devastating*. He played right into the Enemy's hands—not his physical enemy—but the Enemy of his soul. Belshazzar became the Devil's pawn, ultimately giving his physical enemy the victory. God allowed events to unfold that brought Belshazzar's demise that very night as the Persian forces overtook the city and Belshazzar's life was forfeited.

Conduct Yourself Worthy of Your Calling...

I would like for us to ask ourselves some challenging questions while going through this book and to examine our life in light of the Scripture. After all, as Zig Ziglar has said, "If it doesn't challenge you, it won't change you." As believers, our lives are to be set aside for God. We are to conduct ourselves worthy of the calling (Philippians 1:27). We should be challenged to be different than the world. At times for us to be challenged, we need our conscience pricked to be awakened to understand areas in our life where change is needed. The result is to go deeper and realize more from our relationship with Christ.

From Belshazzar's less-than-stellar example, today's believers can learn the importance of understanding who God is and living a God-honoring life. Many people profess to have accepted the gospel message though their acceptance has only changed them to varying degrees. In 2 Corinthians 5:21, Paul was *imploring* (not just asking) believers to be reconciled. As he was writing to the church, he thought some who claimed to be believers [Christians] had been better reconciled than others. Why would we not want to get as much from our relationship with God as possible? Why would we not want to know Him more deeply and live more and more in His presence?

To Know Him Is to Love Him and to Love Him Is to Be Obedient...

The Scripture declares that knowing Christ as our Savior and loving Him results in obedience to Him (1 John 2:3, John 14:15). I don't know about you, but when God looks at me, I want Him to see someone who causes Him to say, "They love me." We must also admit that we will never be able to love God as entirely as He deserves in this sin-tainted flesh, but in our heart, we should hold a propensity toward obedience—though we *may* often miss the mark. The mark of a true believer or a disciple of Christ is to walk in the light as He is in the light (1 John 1:7). We know we can do nothing to earn God's love; we are saved by grace and by nothing that we do. The repentant sinner who knows the great sacrifice Christ made to save him is then compelled to live his life for Him and His glory. The believer is called in Scripture to offer himself to the Lord as a living sacrifice, holy and acceptable. Belshazzar was an ungodly man, yet God held Him responsible for his actions. God expected that the king knew right from wrong and should have acted accordingly; therefore, he reaped what he sowed.

In light of Belshazzar's being responsible for his actions, the author Talbot writes,

> *If God held Belshazzar responsible, my friend, for the ray of light which shone across his pathway, what will He say to men living in the blaze of light which illuminates the world today? Every converted man in this country has more light than Belshazzar had*[2].

Talbot's point is something to consider. God calls the unbeliever to answer to Him, and we, as believers, knowing the truth should be effected. We should desire to live out the gospel to which we so

---
[2] Ibid.

desperately cling and the new life filled with new hopes that it brings. This type of zeal does not come from outward pressures though but solely from within and only from the new birth.

Ephesians 5:8 and 9 tells believers that they were once in darkness, but now they *are* children of light and to live as such in all goodness, righteousness, and truth. In considering these verses and given the account of Belshazzar, there is a serious concern to be had when considering how many confessing believers continue to live, what they seem to value most in life. While Belshazzar was weighed and found wanting, I wonder how many professed believers will also be found wanting? People should see a difference in the life of a believer!

In Hebrews 12:1 Paul's instruction is to "lay aside every weight, and the sin which so easily beset us, and let us run with patience the race that is set before us." In short, salvation leads to a life growing in obedience and spiritual fruit.

I am not saying that we no longer sin after receiving salvation, but I am saying to people who have a true understanding of what Christ did for them, rejecting sin will be no option for them; they will require it of themselves and purpose themselves to live for Christ. Many professed believers have no time for loving or serving God. They reserve all their time to fulfill their desires and wants, to serve and live for themselves. The god many have created in their minds is a god of their design—not the true God. Many have created a god that serves them.

This type of "faith," is seen depicted in 2 Timothy 3. Herein, Paul is addressing Timothy as a teacher and warning against false teachers, saying that many will have a *form* of godliness, but they will not be godly nor have the power of God active in their lives. Instead, they will be lovers of self and living to fulfill the desires of their flesh. He contrasts this to true believers who have an active living faith.

James 1:4 tells the believer to "let patience have perfect work, that ye may be perfect and entire, *wanting* nothing." We must first understand that the phrase, "*let patience,*" does not imply we do nothing. *Strong's Lexicon* says *patience* in this verse means the believer is steadfast and constant; he possesses endurance[3]. Patience is characteristic of a person who does not swerve nor stray but deliberately purposes himself to be loyal, to live faithfully and piously even during intense trials and sufferings. The life of Joseph in the book of Genesis is a prime example of a person who learned to have patience. He was sold into slavery by jealous, vindictive brothers; his master's wife later lied about his supposed attempted violation, which caused him to be imprisoned. Joseph endured many trials that could have embittered him and caused him to forsake his faith; however, he did not allow his struggles keep him from living the life God had appointed for him—to continue persevering in his faith.

Belshazzar and his friends displayed the type of character that a Christian is not supposed to embrace. A Christian should desire to honor God and love God in return for His love. They should desire to serve Christ wholeheartedly, knowing they were dead in their sins before Christ's salvation.

How Will You Be Found?

Before concluding this introduction to this study, I want to finish addressing what happened to Belshazzar this terrible night of judgment. In the midst of his partying, Belshazzar saw something that horrified him! Daniel 5:5-7 records that the event caused his countenance to change, his thoughts were troubled, his legs trembled so violently his knees knocked together. He was so terrified at the sight, he *cried out*.

---

[3] G5281 - hypomonē - Strong's Greek Lexicon (NKJV). Retrieved from https://www.blueletterbible.org//lang/lexicon/lexicon.cfm?Strongs=G5281&t=NKJV

While he could appear to be indifferent about the people for whom he was responsible fighting the great battle ensuing outside the city walls, what God allowed him to see greatly affected him—both emotionally and physically. He saw a hand appear and write four words on the wall: "MENE, MENE, TEKEL, UPHARSIN." The king had no understanding what the words or the dream meant. After the king's advisors failed miserably in interpreting the handwriting, the queen remembered a wise man who could interpret dreams when Nebuchadnezzar had been on the throne. After Daniel was summoned to interpret this message from God, he interpreted the dream and informed Belshazzar that he had been weighed in God's scales and found wanting. That very night when the Persians invaded, Belshazzar, the king of the Chaldeans was killed. Thinking he was safe behind his supposedly impenetrable walls and living his life in opposition to the one true God caused Belshazzar to lose his life.

We too must consider our lives in light of this biblical account. Are we living life in opposition to God? If you will turn to God, humble yourselves, pray and ask for forgiveness for your sins, God will hear you and forgive you. *One day we will all be measured by God's standards—on His scales of justice.* Only those who have accepted Christ and have Him on the scales with them when weighed will be found not wanting. All others will fall short and be cast into hell.

More than having Christ as Savior, believers must also take steps to build their life on the solid foundation of Christ. God deserves for His children to walk humbly before Him because of what Christ did for us and simply because He's God, which is enough reason.

I trust this chapter will remind us all that we have much to lay hold of in Christ. Many believers lack so much of what they can possess from a deeper, more intimate relationship with Christ. He came that we might have life and have it more abundantly (John 10:10). Now is the time to consider Jesus and His will for our lives more sincerely and not to plan Him out of our lives with our choices, daily activities, and godless actions. Otherwise, someday we may discover we drifted far from Him. We need to become better at redeeming the time for the days truly are evil (Ephesians 5:16). Getting caught up in evil or prodigal living can be easy because it comes natural to the flesh.

The Scripture is the basis by which we examine our lives. More specifically, though, this book will use the *Seven Letters to the Seven Churches* found in Revelation chapters 2 and 3 to see how Christ judged the churches—at times bringing commendation, at times rebuke, and at times both. This book is not intended to be an exhaustive verse-by-verse analysis of each letter; rather as a guide to consider the major implications of each letter, the application to the original audience, and then to today's churches. As you go through this study, consider the modern churches and how they fare in comparison. Likewise, consider your faith in contrast.

Keep the following questions in mind as you study each chapter and then complete the study guide at each chapter's end.

- For what did Christ commend the church (if anything)? The commendations should encourage and help us to understand what Christ looks for in His church.

- For what did Christ rebuke the church for (if anything)? Christ's rebuke should cause us to reflect.

- In examining our lives against the rebuke, do we need to change?

- What was the warning or what could happen as a result of the troubled area not being mended?

- Do you see any of the areas addressed that need to be corrected as being problematic in the modern church?

Introduction

Jesus Letter to You

Consider this additional question: if Jesus were to write *you* a letter, what would it say? I believe this excellent question should be kept in mind as we may be able to identify with several aspects of the letters that require correction or at the very least, from which we need to distance ourselves. Two concepts from Scripture apply when looking at these letters:

1. Proverbs 4:23 declares, "Keep your heart with all diligence, For out of it spring the issues of life."

2. Psalm 139:23-24 proclaims, "Search me, O God, and know my heart; Try me, and know my anxieties; And see if there is any wicked way in me, and lead me in the way everlasting."

We must have an open heart to God's leading.

In our lives and churches, we must always stand for truth and be willing to change where change is needed. Prayerfully approach this study with a reliance on the Holy Spirit's guidance and an open heart to let Christ do a work in you when and where needed. You have everything to gain, and perhaps everything to lose to do otherwise.

1

Ephesus— the Loveless Church

"To the angel of the church of Ephesus write, "These things says He who holds the seven stars in His right hand, who walks in the midst of the seven golden lampstands: I know your works, your labor, your patience, and that you cannot bear those who are evil. And you have tested those who say they are apostles and are not, and have found them liars; and you have persevered and have patience, and have labored for My name's sake and have not become weary. Nevertheless I have this against you, that you have left your first love. Remember therefore from where you have fallen; repent and do the first works, or else I will come to you quickly and remove your lampstand from its place—unless you repent. But this you have, that you hate the deeds of the Nicolaitans, which I also hate. He who has an ear, let him hear what the Spirit says to the churches. To him who overcomes I will give to eat from the tree of life, which is in the midst of the Paradise of God."

(Revelation 2:1-7)

1

Ephesus— the Loveless Church

(Revelation 2:1-7)

One day I received a call from a lady who attended our church. Seemingly distraught, she asked if I could stop by and talk with her. Later that day, my wife and I stopped to visit her. When I asked her how we could help, tears began to stream down her face. "Pastor," she stated in a weakened voice, "words on paper...just words on paper! For nearly all my adult life, I have served and have been zealous for God, but lately, I have no zeal. I am numb to Him. I read my Bible, and they are just words on paper—no more meaningful to me than any other writing. I don't seem to have the heart for God or others I know I should and want. What do I need to do?" She desired to have the love for God and others that she once remembered. I took a moment to pray with her then I reassured her she was in a much better place than she knew!

Why was this dear lady in a better place than she knew? She realized her lack and then need. Too many seem to have their love for God and others wax cold without any concern or a desire to take corrective actions. At least she remembered and desired to have the zeal and love for God and others back that she so fondly remembered.

The real problem is when people do not realize this is where they are in their faith and take no steps to correct the problem. With a heart for revival, she was indeed in a perfect place to get back to where she wanted and needed to be.

If many people were to take some time for self-examination and were being honest with themselves, I believe they could admit they have lost their zeal for the Lord and seeing others saved. If they were honest, they might tell you they are happy as they are, not wanting to put forth more energy to grow in what they know of God. They become indifferent to sharing the gospel with others, mainly leaving the task of sharing the gospel to others. They have grown comfortable with where they are and how things are in their life.

This lackadaisical, indifferent attitude is a reason for concern that could have significant consequences. The problem that plagued the church at Ephesus is a problem that affects many in the church today. Before delving deeper into the specific problems of each church, I want to help you better understand the challenges of the world in which they lived.

A Short History of Ephesus

Ephesus in Bible times was a major seaport and center of commerce and trade when the letters to the churches in Revelation were written. With a population of approximately 250,000, this prominent city was considered one of the seven wonders of the ancient world. The church at Ephesus was likewise prominent due to those who served there: the apostle Paul and Timothy; Aquila, Priscilla and Apollos; and even John, the writer of Revelation[4]. Imagine the preaching and teaching that was taking place there! From our viewpoint, we might wonder

---

[4]Guzik, D. "Study Guide for Revelation 2 by David Guzik." Blue Letter Bible. Last Modified 21 Feb, 2017. https://www.blueletter-bible.org/Comm/guzik_david/StudyGuide2017-Rev/Rev-2.cfm

how the people could have strayed from the faith in any way with these great teachers serving them. However, they did—just as we do in areas.

Many false religions were being practiced and many false gods were being worshipped in the city of Ephesus. The city flaunted glorious temples to false gods. One such temple constructed in honor of Diana, the fertility goddess, was so massive, 127 sixty-foot-tall pillars supported the edifice. The temple was located at the theater in Ephesus, which was also an imposing complex capable of holding 25,000 spectators[5]. Acts 19:23-41 records the account of a mob being incited against Paul because his ministry was considered a threat to Diana worship.

History records that the temple of Diana was a major treasury and bank. The assets of merchants, kings, and cities were deposited there with the belief that their monies would be protected by the goddess. Imagine the degree to which this corrupt system had a hold on their society. Ephesus was a major stronghold of Satan.

You may be wondering how this history of Ephesus pertains to you or benefits you. To more richly appreciate that the early church faced some of the same struggles as we do and sometimes maybe to a worse degree is essential in understanding the challenges of the early church. These pressures likely caused some to fall away from the church and others to grow weary in their faith—the same as pressures from today's society causes many to fall away. Many went through all the motions, yet they lacked compassion in their work. We should be encouraged to know that Christ declared the early church believers could do something about this attitude and overcome what they faced in their environment. Likewise, we can too.

---

[5] Ibid.

Jesus Commends the Church of Ephesus

In the introduction of His letter, Jesus commended the church for all they were doing in His name. Jesus said He knew their works—as He knows what we do in the church and in our personal lives. The church worked to be doctrinally pure and was active in the ministry of Christ. Looking in from the outside would reveal a solid church that worked diligently. Some important lessons are included in this commendation for church members:

- Be active.

- Test the teachings of others.

- Never stand for evil.

- Be patient.

- Do not grow weary in doing good.

The Church of Ephesus was an active church that took their faith seriously, but the church also faced a big problem that Christ addressed. The Son of God first commended them but then came the correction. We can learn much from His example in handling the correction. Noting the good people do is honorable, but the areas that need correcting must not be glazed over or neglected.

When looking at the rebuke brought to this church by Jesus, reflect on the following questions:

1) What area needed to be addressed in this church?

2) What can we learn from this church's condemnation to improve on our own walk of faith?

Jesus Rebukes the Church of Ephesus

In Revelation 4:2, Jesus states, "Nevertheless I have this against you, that you have left your first love." While much speculation has been written on whether this rebuke refers to their loving God as they first did or others as they should, I believe this letter deals more with the attitude or passion with which they approached their faith, including their fervor toward both God and others.

Jesus had already commended them for their devotion to God, proper doctrine and personal obedience. But what they lacked was not *quantity* but *quality* in what motivated them to act on their faith. The Ephesians were praised for their labor, for their patient endurance, and for their resistance to false teachers—the Nicolaitans. The people were busy doing the work, but the heart from which their labor flowed was not a heart that was zealous for God. Introducing others to the saving grace of God came more from a sense of duty. They did the work of God out of obligation, feeling they had to because that is what was expected of them. This church was not lukewarm in their faith, but the people were on their way to becoming a lukewarm church if something didn't change. Implied in Jesus warning them that He would remove His lampstand if they did not repent.

In essence, 1 Corinthians 13:1 declares that if we do not love, what good does anything else profit us? Many people need to deeply consider this truth today. The love declared by many is not the reality of how they truly feel in their heart. Their love, which does not last outside the four walls of the church, does not permeate their life. This is sad as loving others is an essential mark of a believer (John 13:35). Christ's children are to treat others with care and compassion by feeding the hungry, giving drink to the thirsty, clothing the naked, visiting the sick and those in prison (Matthew 25:34-36). The Ephesians were not lacking in their work; rather, their good works flowed from a heart deficient of unconditional love.

In today's vernacular, a catchphrase could be applied to the Ephesians: they were experiencing burnout. The people were going through the motions, but the excitement and zeal had worn off. Please don't misunderstand me. None of us will always feel like doing what we should as believers, but we can't see ourselves doing anything other than serving God. We are glad to serve Him because of what we have in Christ, and we do want others to have the same hope we do. The Ephesians were still doing good, but their heart was no longer in their service. Their motivation did not come from a heart that truly loved God and others. Jesus wanted the people to hold a correct attitude.

How to Overcome

The first instruction Christ tells the church is to remember (Revelation 2:4-5). In remembering, the people could reflect upon how Christ had redeemed them. Remember when you first came to realize how hopeless you were in your sin and unable to save yourself? Remember the love that Christ showed toward you while you were still a sinner by dying for your sins on the cross? Remember how much Christ sacrificed for your salvation? Remember the joy you first had in Christ and your desire to share it with others? That is the call in this verse—for believers to remember how they had once rejoiced at their newfound faith and showed true *agape* love to others.

Do you remember the zeal you had when first saved? I believe nearly everyone would consider that day of reckoning an exciting time. How could we do less than rejoice upon realizing our fate because of sin and how Christ saved us from the consequences of our sin by dying on the cross in our place and taking the penalty for our sin on Himself! This newfound faith gave us the zeal to learn more about God and to share it with others so they could enjoy what we had.

Christ was pointing the Ephesian people to remember this enthusiasm. Christ called the Ephesians to repent and return and to do this work again. Considering what Christ went through on our behalf, not to have a correct appreciation and adoration for Christ is sinful.

For this very reason, the lady who sought counsel for feeling only numbness toward serving God was in such a good place. She remembered what she had once experienced and wanted to embrace that love or zeal she first had for God and others.

By considering God's great love for them and Christ's finished work on the cross, the believers would be compelled to return to their first love. The Scripture warns that, in the end times, the love of many will wax cold because of lawlessness (Matthew 24:12). People are becoming more concerned with living for the desires of their sinful flesh and losing their focus and heart for what is truly important.

Matthew 24:37-39 contains excellent words of wisdom for every believer today.

> As the days of Noah were, so also will the coming of the Son of man be. For as in the days before the flood they were eating and drinking, marrying and giving in marriage, until the day that Noah entered the ark, and did not know until the flood came and took them all away, so also will the coming of the Son of man be.

The people were living it up, ignoring the warning until it was too late. Today's Christians must NOT make this same mistake! Like Belshazzar, many will not heed the call to turn to God and repent. As believers, we need to continually nurture our relationship with Christ and never forget what a gift we have received in salvation and the great sacrifice required to save us. We must never lose heart! We serve because we are thrilled at what we received in Christ and desire for others to have this saving faith. We must also keep focused, and while it is daylight, we must tell others about the good news of Christ!

When Jesus went to the cross, He told His disciples "unless a grain of wheat falls into the ground and dies it remains alone; BUT if it dies it produces much grain" (John 12:24). This guarantee is why the church must remember what is truly important—their first love. Remind yourself and return to your first love as often as is necessary. With a zeal Christ is worthy of, be committed to love God and love others.

Seven Letters Study Guide
Chapter 1 — The Church at Ephesus

1. For what did Christ commend the church (if anything)? The commendations should encourage us to acquire these attributes desired in the Christian's life.

2. For what did Christ rebuke the church (if anything)? Christ's rebuke should cause us to reflect and examine our own life against the rebuke. Do we need change?

    B. What was the warning or what could happen as a result of the troubled area not being addressed and mended?

3. Do you see any of the areas covered that need corrected as being problematic in the modern church? If so, what corrective action needs to be taken?

4. What additional thoughts came to mind when reviewing this letter? What else could have been highlighted or could we learn from the church of Ephesus?

2

Smyrna—
The Poor/Persecuted Church

And to the angel of the church in Smyrna write, "These things says the First and the Last, who was dead, and came to life: I know your works, tribulation, and poverty (but you are rich); and I know the blasphemy of those who say they are Jews and are not, but are a synagogue of Satan. Do not fear any of those things which you are about to suffer. Indeed, the devil is about to throw some of you into prison, that you may be tested, and you will have tribulation ten days. Be faithful until death, and I will give you the crown of life. He who has an ear, let him hear what the Spirit says to the churches. He who overcomes shall not be hurt by the second death."

(Revelation 2:8-11)

2

Smyrna— The Poor/Persecuted Church

(Revelation 2:8-11)

The date was AD 155. Christians in the town of Smyrna were under great persecution by the Romans who had annexed the land. The pressure they were under was only intensified by Jewish believers who saw the Christians as a threat and sought to have them eradicated. Polycarp, one of the early church leaders, was arrested and taken to the arena, where he was ordered to repent of his belief in Christ. A crowd had gathered to watch the man repent and instead give preference to Caesar. When he refused to betray his Savior, he was again urged to denounce Christ and be set free.

"Consider your age, Polycarp," the 86-year-old preacher of the gospel was told. "Make it easy on yourself! Just worship Caesar and, in doing so, deny Christ, and you can go!"

But the words of Jesus recorded in Revelation 2:10 reflected the heart of Polycarp: "Be faithful until death, and I will give you the crown of life." Polycarp had no interest in being freed by men if it meant renouncing the eternal freedom he had received in Christ. In faith, he took Jesus at His word, knowing no person, no Devil—nothing could separate him from Christ. And Polycarp was not about to separate himself!

As the threats continued for him to renounce Christ or die, Polycarp declared, "How can I blaspheme my God and my Savior? You threaten me with fire that burns for an hour and is over. But the judgment on the ungodly is forever[6]."

With his hands tied behind his back, he was fastened to a stake. Polycarp looked toward heaven and prayed to his Lord and Savior as the wood piled around him was set ablaze. History records that as the fire blazed furiously, a miracle happened. Onlookers were amazed to see that the flames did not touch the aged Polycarp. Those responsible for his execution finally conceded that the flames would not consume him and therefore ordered an executioner to stab Polycarp with a dagger[7]. The man of God died from the injury, but in perfect peace knowing his final fate was up to no man but secured in Christ.

In this letter from Christ, the church of Smyrna was epitomized in the life and death of Polycarp. Though persecuted, he endured until the end. Polycarp understood eternal life was only because of Christ, and revering God, who not only could take the physical life but also determine a person's eternity was better than fearing mankind who could only take the physical life.

Polycarp needed nothing in his present life but his faith to endure through any trial or tribulation. What about you? Do you understand what Polycarp understood? This man of God faced the ultimate challenge of an agonizing death because of his faith. How do you respond in the face of adversity, even in the smaller trials of life: fear or faith? Our faith will be challenged by the letter to the church at Smyrna to see if our faith and expectations of the Christian faith line up with the faith of people willing to face the executioner.

---

[6] "Polycarp's Martyrdom." Christian History Institute, christianhistoryinstitute.org/study/module/polycarp/.
[7] Ibid.

If we have nothing else in this life but Christ, is He enough? Are we content only to have Him?

He [Jesus] Knows

A central theme throughout the *Seven Letters* is that nothing is hidden from Jesus. We learn in Revelation 2:9 that Jesus knows the work, tribulation, and poverty of those in the church of Smyrna. I want to ask the question from the introduction again: "*What letter would Jesus write when looking at your Christian walk?*" He knows you better than you know yourself. What would Christ say over you? How would He say you handle the tribulations in your life? How content are you *with what you have* in this life?

When Jesus looked at the lives of those in the church at Smyrna, He commended and encouraged them. The believers at Smyrna were one of only two churches for which Christ had no rebuke. Though those attending the church in Smyrna were greatly persecuted and poor, they kept going in their faith and received Jesus' commendation. They didn't hear His words of rebuke for the church members at Ephesus for their ritualistic service that lacked love. THOUGH persecuted and poor, they still had a zeal for Jesus in their lives that they extended to others!

The letter to Smyrna debunks many false teachings. I have heard preachers and teachers say every Christian should be rich and have their heart's desire—material possessions, healing, and so forth. A common teaching spreading among Christians is the person who lacks wealth or health has a faith problem; the person is not exercising enough faith or claiming for himself what he has received in Christ.

The letter to Smyrna tells a different story: there is no guarantee of wealth or health in this world. Trials will come in this world (John 16:33). The world hated Christ and will also hate those who are followers of Him (John 15:18). Whether we abound or are abased (Philippians 4:12) or have a little or a lot is not always tied directly to our faith, or lack thereof. We are to be content in our faith—no matter what circumstances we face as we walk this earth.

If the persecution or lack of wealth in the church of Smyrna had anything to do with a deficiency in their faith, Christ would have rebuked them. But Christ had no rebuke for this church, which corrects those who teach false or unbalanced teachings of health and wealth, and as such, this letter can be used to discern false teachers of the faith.

The question that remains is why would a loving God allow His children to suffer?

The Joy of Persecution

In James 1:2-4, the believer is instructed to "count it all joy when you fall into various trials, knowing that the testing of your faith produces patience. But let patience have her perfect work, that you may be perfect and complete, lacking nothing." God can use our trials to grow us spiritually. They allow us the opportunity to practice our faith by turning to Him and trusting in Him. That the name *Smyrna* also means "myrrh[8]" seems to be no coincidence. Myrrh, an essential oil derived from certain trees, is commonly used as a perfume and even in the embalming of bodies. The myrrh essential oil possesses several health benefits from serving as an antiseptic to containing anti-inflammatory properties[9]. In the ancient world, myrrh had value because of its multiple uses. Myrrh is mentioned numerous times in the Bible—as a

---

[8]Bell, G. (2017). How Good Is Good Enough for God?. [online] Google Books. Available at: https://books.google.com/books [Accessed 18 May 2019].

[9]Cohen, J. (2019). A Wise Man's Cure: Frankincense and Myrrh. [online] HISTORY. Available at: https://www.history.com/news/a-wise-mans-cure-frankincense-and-myrrh [Accessed 28 Aug. 2019].

perfume, as a component of the incense God instructed Moses to use in the tabernacle services, as one of the gifts the wise men brought to Mary upon Jesus' birth, and when mixed with wine and offered to Christ on the cross.

To harvest this valuable commodity, the tree had to be injured or scarred. Those who collected the resin and sap would then tightly wrap the wound in the tree, pressing the myrrh resin from the tree. The word *persecuted* means "pressed." Without "evangelistically speaking," I find it interesting to consider all these meanings together regarding the plight of those at Smyrna. I believe that during the times of hardship the people faced, they used their persecution as an opportunity to trust God and something beneficial came from that trust—faith. They may have had scars from all that they endured in this world, but what they had more of than trouble was faith in Christ! What came forth from them being scarred and pressed was faith. What an excellent analogy to help us remember their plight!

The hard times in life can be used as a springboard to grow our faith and then benefit from them. Many often do exactly the opposite, and as a result of the trials, they are drawn away or fall away from their faith. Their trials could have been a reason to rejoice as they grew more Christ-like through the hard times. In Christ their battle was already won, and through their faithful response, they were then deeply rooted and grounded in the faith. Their faithfulness and trust in Him rose as a sweet-smelling aroma/incense before God.

How about you? How you respond to trials demonstrates how deeply rooted and grounded you are in your faith. Do you trust God or respond in fear? When we fear we forfeit the rest Christ died for and desires for every believer to have. When we react in faith and trust Christ, no matter the circumstance, we can rest in His faithfulness!

Hard-pressed on Every Side

From where did this persecution on all sides arise? Their tribulation came at the hand of the occupying government. The people were expected to worship the ruler of the occupying nation, but they refused. Those who attended the church at Smyrna lived in a society with tremendous cultural pressure to worship other gods; they refused. Tribulation also came from the Jews who brought much persecution on them through their influence on society. This persecution levied on their own people led Christ to refer to them as a "house of Satan" and declared them guilty of blasphemy (Revelation 2:9). In other words, when they spoke or done evil to those of the church in Smyrna, they were doing likewise to Christ. These strong words of condemnation from Christ let the Jews know they were in direct opposition to Him!

Because Jesus had no rebuke for the church of Smyrna, we can rightly ascertain they loved and had a zeal for Christ. They did not let their persecution become a stumbling block; **to the world they were poor, but in Spirit, they were rich beyond measure**.

2 Corinthians 4:8-9 comes to my mind, which states, "We are hard-pressed on every side, but not crushed; perplexed, but not in despair; persecuted, but not abandoned; struck down but not destroyed."

The Christians were hard-pressed, but they did not let it affect their faith! Being faith filled was simple to them; they had every spiritual blessing in the heavenlies (Ephesians 1:3) in Christ. The believers refused to let the enemy take the joy of their salvation from them no matter the tribulation! Jesus encouraged them to continue in their faith to the end when they would receive the crown of life! I am reminded of Paul's words in Romans 8:18 that explains to us that the troubles of this world are not even worthy of comparing the glory that awaits those in Christ.

Two Commands to Follow.

We tend to complicate matters in life, don't we? The call of God is simple: know Him and trust Him! His simple call of "remain faithful" was embraced by the church at Smyrna. Yes, the battle can be fierce, which is why we must rely on the strength of God and heed the call of Ephesians 6 to put on the full armor of God.

The author John Maxwell reminds us that too many Christians have uphill hopes but downhill habits! To endure or persevere successfully in the faith is to respond in faith and not lose our peace or simple trust in Christ through worry, anxiety or fear. One produces good results in our life while the other brings havoc. Our call is to be faithful in the completed work of Christ! If those in Smyrna could stay faithful in Christ, so can we! Their comfort came from knowing Christ, who they were in Christ, and not letting any person, devil, or situation steal the hope of their salvation.

1 John 5:4 declares, "Whatever is born of God overcomes the world. And this is the victory that has overcome the world—our faith!" This attitude is what we see in the patriarch Job when he declares, "I don't know the *why* to everything, but I know my Redeemer lives, and one day I will behold Him with these very eyes" (Job 19:25-27). The call is not to let anything rob you of your security in Christ because He is worth it! And though this letter was written to the church at Smyrna, it contains an individual message for every believer: remain faithful.

The Old Testament bears record of how life became difficult for the Israelites when they murmured and began to be drawn away by their emotions. As a result, they became unfaithful. Exodus 14 addresses the account of the Israelites' arrival at the Red Sea after being freed from Egypt. The Red Sea in front of them appears impassable, unscalable cliffs are on each side of them, and the Egyptian army is closing in from behind to retake and return them. The children of Israel cried out to God, but His unimaginable response was for them to stop crying and move forward in their faith, in the word of God, and in the promise He had already given.

He had already promised He would take them to the Promised Land and give them the land of promise. Did they have the faith to get there? God has likewise promised us He can deliver us, be with us, and successfully see us to the end. Do we have the confidence in Him to get there? "Stop crying! Go forward!" would be the call to those frozen in fear instead of only moving forward in faith and in the simple trust of God to fulfill His Word. We must remember God cannot lie. If He said He would, He will.

Faith is not the absence of problems; the Word of God promises we will have tribulation. 2 Timothy 3:10 states that "all who desire to live godly in Christ Jesus will suffer persecution." The Israelites had a legitimate problem: they were caught between the enemy and the Red Sea. Those at Smyrna like Polycarp had real-life troubles: they were being persecuted by the authorities. On earth we all will have tribulation, but we are called to live above the problem. Because Polycarp and those in Smyrna responded in faith, the trials of life ultimately had no power over them! We can either give the Enemy or Christ the control over our lives. Christ had already won the victory, so in Him, we are more than conquerors as we walk in the victory He already secured for us.

1 Peter 5:10 declares "May the God of all grace, who called us to His eternal glory by Christ Jesus, after you have suffered a while, perfect, establish, strengthen, and settle you."

So, I leave you with this last thought: examine yourself. Who or what have you given the power to rule in your life? Your circumstances or your faith? The flesh, the enemy of your soul, or God.

Seven Letters Study Guide
Chapter 2 — The Church at Smyrna

1. For what did Christ commend the church (if anything)? The commendations should encourage us to acquire these attributes desired in the Christian's life.

2. For what did Christ rebuke the church for (if anything)? Christ's rebuke should cause us to reflect and examine our own life against the rebuke. Do we need change?

   B. What was the warning or what could happen as a result of the troubled area not being addressed and mended?

3. Do you see any of the areas covered that need corrected as being problematic in the modern church? If so, what corrective action needs to be taken?

4. What additional thoughts came to mind when reviewing this letter? What else could have been highlighted or could we learn from the church at Smyrna?

3

Pergamos—
The Compromising Church

And to the angel of the church in Pergamos write, "These things says He who has the sharp two-edged sword: I know your works, and where you dwell, where Satan's throne is. And you hold fast to My name, and did not deny My faith even in the days in which Antipas was My faithful martyr, who was killed among you, where Satan dwells. But I have a few things against you, because you have there those who hold the doctrine of Balaam, who taught Balak to put a stumbling block before the children of Israel, to eat things sacrificed to idols, and to commit sexual immorality. Thus you also have those who hold the doctrine of the Nicolaitans, which thing I hate. Repent, or else I will come to you quickly and will fight against them with the sword of My mouth. He who has an ear, let him hear what the Spirit says to the churches. To him who overcomes I will give some of the hidden manna to eat. And I will give him a white stone, and on the stone a new name written which no one knows except him who receives it."

(Revelation 2:12-17)

3

Pergamos— The Compromising Church

(Revelation 2:12-17)

The seven letters to the seven churches found in Revelation chapters 2-3, which were written in AD 96, were not written solely for the churches in that age but for admonition and encouragement to churches throughout the ages, i.e., for us. These lessons continue to be crucial for today's churches.

The first letter addressed the church at Ephesus, and while the people were persistent in the faith and did not endure false teachings, they were waxing cold in their love and were at risk of becoming lukewarm. The second letter to the church at Smyrna addressed how the people were suffering great persecution and were encouraged to endure to the end. The people may have been poor by the world's standards, when, in fact, they were rich beyond measure in Christ. This chapter will examine the third letter to the church at Pergamos.

Pergamos was a city located about 65 miles north of Smyrna with a population of approximately 190,000 inhabitants. Like those in Ephesus and Smyrna, Pergamos also was home to several grand temples built for the worship of false gods. Additionally, Pergamos was the capital of the Roman Empire's province in Asia and the center of worship to Caesar[10]. Revelation 3:13 mentions this was the very place where Satan dwelt. These facts illustrate the enormous magnitude of evil, temptation and persecution the church faced.

Their Profession: Believers of Christ

Considering the multiple challenges the church faced, Christ commended them for being faithful in holding to and proclaiming the name of Jesus as Savior. Though they lived in a city that held no regard for Christ, instead worshiping false gods and Caesar, and though greatly persecuted for their faith, they embraced the name of Christ. In so doing, they risked martyrdom, and some were martyred simply for refusing to deny the name of Christ. However, though they were zealous enough in their faith to be crucified for what they believed, they did not crucify their own flesh. They were not completely in practice what they were in profession.

Their Practice: Compromising

In practice, some in the church at Pergamos fell short. Verses 14 and 15 reveal that they were falling short in being obedient in their faith. Their sins were like those Balaam taught Balak in order to cause the children of Israel to stumble, and for some at Pergamos to live like the Nicolaitans. What exactly did Christ mean with His censure? In the story of Balaam (Numbers 22-31), the king of the Moabites was scared of the Israelites. He had heard what God had done for the Israelites in Egypt. As a result, the king wanted them to be cursed so they would lose their effectiveness. Likewise, we have an Enemy who also knows what God can do through those committed to living their lives for God's glory. For this very reason, the Enemy comes to

---

[10]Minnesota, D. (2009). Revelation – Page 9 – Pursuing Truth. [online] Pursuing Truth. Available at: https://adammaarschalk.com/category/revelation/page/9/ [Accessed 16 Feb. 2017].

steal, kill, and destroy (John 10:10). The Enemy's goal for God's people throughout history has been to bring destruction—especially in issues relating to their Christian character and witness. The Enemy accomplished this goal in the church at Pergamos.

To continue the story in Numbers of Balaam and Balak, the Enemy had no power to curse God's people. Instead, the Enemy brought about their downfall by persuading them to compromise—failing to be completely faithful. They practiced many of the same forms of idolatry and sexually immoral activities as the Moabites. In short, they professed to be "God's people", but tended to live like the rest of the world.

They abandoned honoring God in many areas of their lives and the pursuit of holy living. In practicing the same sins as the Moabites, they lost much of their identity as a distinctive people of God - and in turn also became tolerant. As they became so ingrained in the Moabite society, they would likewise not want to fight against them. The enemy could not curse or bring destruction on them but they could themselves – by choosing their idols over God.

Consider someone calling themselves a believer, but when others look at them, their focus and desires in life largely appear no different than anyone else – with little or no change in their life. What they seem to be focused on is not lifting up Christ's standards [holy living] but their own interests. How effective would or could such believers be in the ministry or in being a witness for Christ? Because of compromise leading to idolatry (putting their own pet interests above God's) or any true difference in their life over what the world had to offer, many at Pergamos were struggling.

Many "believers" hold the same attitude as those Christ warns at Pergamos. They profess Christ but in reality are not sincere in their pursuit to seek more of Christ or to live by His Spirit - instead continuing to live by the desires of the flesh (putting their idols first and committing or becoming indifferent to sexual immorality). What is important to God does not appear to be more important to them than living as they want. Nor does pointing others to Christ for salvation seem to concern them deeply. And, because of how they live they could struggle with credibility.

For their actions, Christ warned those at Pergamos that He Himself would fight against them (v. 16). Consider the implications of this warning. When our actions cause us to be in opposition to Christ, the results can be nothing less than unsettling as they cause us to be in a battle of wills with God who cannot lose. Our arms are too short to box with God!

Much of their shortcomings or compromise probably resulted from merely neglecting or not being fully committed to know and then accept nothing less than God's Word as their standard for living. They likely possessed no more than a basic knowledge of God's Word. When God's people are committed to know God *and* be faithful, the victory is theirs! The Word of God validates the fact that the Enemy has no power over God's people unless given to him. Romans 8:7 declares we are "more than conquerors through Him who loved us." James 4:7 and 8 states, "Submit yourselves therefore to God. Resist the devil, and he will flee from you." These two verses encompass the victory and status we already have and can enjoy as children of God.

Those at Pergamos needed to know God through His Word and not allow the Enemy to cause them to stumble or have less than what they could in Christ. How about us as believers? Do we live below the life Christ died for us to obtain? Do we know who God is through His Word? Are we committed to live our life for His glory? Where do we give the Enemy a place in our life?

The problem those at Pergamos experienced still remains a considerable problem in today's church. That problem could be exacerbated with our lack of knowledge. The theologian Albert Mohler wrote about this problem in an article titled "The Scandal of Biblical Illiteracy: It's Our Problem[11]."

In this article Dr. Mohler addresses how extensive the problem of biblical ignorance is in the church. Regardless of who conducts the poll or who gathers and interprets the statistics, and the general pattern remains the same. Researchers, George Gallup and Jim Castelli, report: "Americans revere the Bible but, by and large, they do not read it. And, because they don't read it, they have become a nation of biblical illiterates." According to the statistics, the problem is more significant than many could begin to imagine. Fewer than half of all adults can name the four gospels. Many Christians cannot identify more than two or three of the disciples. According to the Barna Research Group, sixty percent of Americans can't list five of the Ten Commandments. How are people to be affected by the Ten Commandments if they do not know them[12]?

To further demonstrate the problem of biblical illiteracy, one Barna poll revealed that at least twelve percent of adults believe Joan of Arc was Noah's wife. Another survey showed that over half of these polled thought Sodom and Gomorrah were husband and wife. In light of this alarming data, Mohler states rather succinctly, "We are in big trouble[13]." The fact that we live at a time when more people likely know the names of the "Fab Four" (the Beatles) than the names of the twelve disciples betrays the desperate need to get into the Word.

In considering how little Scripture people know, Mohler says, "No wonder Christians show a growing tendency to compromise..." In reference to the church, he continues, "This [biblical illiteracy] really

---

[11] Mohler, A. (2016). The Scandal of Biblical Illiteracy: It's Our Problem. [online] Albertmohler.com. Available at: https://albertmohler.com/2016/01/20/the-scandal-of-biblical-illiteracy-its-our-problem-4/
[12] Ibid.
[13] Ibid.

is our problem, and it is up to this generation of Christians to reverse course[14]." The implications of this need not only affect the church body but also how effective the church is in changing society for good.

God addresses this very topic in the fifth chapter of Isaiah when disclosing why His people were going into captivity: "My people have gone into captivity, because they have no knowledge; Their honorable men are famished, and their multitude dried up with thirst" (v. 5). Verse 24b adds, "Because they have rejected the law of the LORD of hosts, and despised the word" as further cause for their plight. God makes plain that their troubles were due to their willful disobedience and neglect of Him and His Word. In short, we need to know God's Word better than we currently do as a body of believers if the Bible is to affect our lives in a meaningful way.

Mohler expounds on the fact that believers need to know the Scripture in order to experience needed change and then be able to live on the high road of holiness. To combat this problem of biblical illiteracy, more people must begin reading and studying the Word and their church authorities must focus on the need for biblical knowledge in the homes of their church members' families and ministries. The bigger picture involves believers' understanding that we are called to be disciples ourselves and then become part of the process of producing more disciples; this is the command of the Great Commission found in Matthew 28.

Repentance: Their only Hope

Revelation 2:16 contained a strong warning that Christ Himself, using His Word, would fight against those at Pergamos unless they repented. The phrase, "using His word" could signify more than simply bringing strong corrective and convicting teachings; the warning could be

---

[14] Ibid.

inclusive of any or all the warnings in Scripture for indulging in various sins. The consequences that could come to fruition for ignoring the Words of a Holy God could be devastating.

All the people had to do was REPENT! To see the problem, agree with God, and walk in His ways. The call of God is for every believer to be in practice what he is in profession—not by our strength or for our good. Yes, we have to put forth some effort, which, yes, is good for us, but ultimately, change only comes by the power of the Holy Spirit as we yield to Him and is for the glory of God as we lift Him up in our lives. If we walk by the Spirit, we will not fulfill the lust of the flesh, and in the Spirit, we cannot lose!

The call of Ephesians 6:10 is to be strong *in the Lord*, and the power of HIS might—His power and strength—NOT ours! If we will don His armor, we cannot lose, for He has already won the battle and, in Him, we are more than victors! The rest of Christ, which is mentioned in Hebrews 4, is for those who believe in Him; however, this rest only comes from having a faith that results in faithfulness not only to understanding but also living out the Word. The rest comes as what we profess becomes the reality of our lives.

I ask you today, for what are you living? Your desires only or for the glory of God? For Christ who gave His life to save you? Do you realize today that you were bought with a great price? That price was the life of Christ! Do you recognize the staggering price that Christ paid? If you genuinely do, that awareness will change your desires and ultimately change you. Maybe today you need to be reminded of the problem that infiltrated the church at Pergamos, and you also need to repent. Christ gave this message to the church at Pergamos: repent!

Overcome!

We must be watchful that in our lives, we don't miss the blessing of discipline. We must not lose touch of being salt and light in a dark world. Balaam tried to erase the line of distinction between God's people and the world, and our Enemy who fights against God's plans still uses this age-old tactic. We must be committed to raising high the name of Christ.

The Promises

He that overcomes shall be given to eat of the hidden manna. While many live mainly to satisfy the desires of their flesh, living by the flesh is never truly satisfying to a child of God and only the manna that comes from God as promised in Revelation 2 satisfies. Only a life set apart for Him and living life in the light of His presence (and what He wills for us) satisfies the soul that longs to be more and more united to his Creator with this promise ultimately fulfilled in the eternal life received in Him. Their new name will be engraved on a white stone showing the permanence of what they received. Those who belong to Christ, as evidenced by their confession of faith and through the fruits of repentance, will forever live in the presence of Christ. What a promise for us to lay hold of today!

Seven Letters Study Guide
Chapter 3 — The Church at Pergamos

1. For what did Christ commend the church (if anything)? The commendations should encourage us to acquire these attributes desired in the Christian's life.

2. For what did Christ rebuke the church for (if anything)? Christ's rebuke should cause us to reflect and examine our own life against the rebuke. Do we need change?

    B. What was the warning or what could happen as a result of the troubled area not being addressed and mended?

3. Do you see any of the areas covered that need corrected as being problematic in the modern church? If so, what corrective action needs to be taken?

4. What additional thoughts came to mind when reviewing this letter? What else could have been highlighted or could we learn from the church at Pergamos?

4

Thyatira—
The Corrupt Church

And to the angel of the church in Thyatira write, "These things says the Son of God, who has eyes like a flame of fire, and His feet like fine brass: I know your works, love, service, faith, and your patience; and as for your works, the last are more than the first. Nevertheless, I have a few things against you, because you allow that woman Jezebel, who calls herself a prophetess, to teach and seduce My servants to commit sexual immorality and eat things sacrificed to idols. And I gave her time to repent of her sexual immorality, and she did not repent. Indeed I will cast her into a sickbed, and those who commit adultery with her into great tribulation, unless they repent of their deeds. I will kill her children with death, and all the churches shall know that I am He who searches the minds and hearts. And I will give to each one of you according to your works. Now to you I say, and to the rest in Thyatira, as many as do not have this doctrine, who have not known the depths of Satan, as they say, I will put on you no other burden. But hold fast what you have till I come. And he who overcomes, and keeps My works until the end, to him I will give power over the nations— "He shall rule them with a rod of iron; They shall be dashed to pieces like the potter's vessels"— as I also have received from My Father; and I will give him the morning star. He who has an ear, let him hear what the Spirit says to the churches."

(Revelation 2:18-29)

4

Thyatira— The Corrupt Church

(Revelation 2:18-29)

When those who call themselves believers compromise (as troubling as it is) that is one matter, yet even more troublesome is when church leaders and teachers adopt and approve of sin. We live in a time when many churches are not only turning a blind eye to sin but are endorsing it as being acceptable, i.e., abortion and same-gender marriage. The letter to the church of Thyatira addresses such issues, and this important message contains a strong warning to those to whom this category applies. But for those who were not in accord with such foolishness and blatant dishonor to God, the letter contains a message of encouragement. This letter reminds us again that we can remain at peace no matter how bad the world seems, knowing Christ reigns above all and ultimately, in the end, He will receive all the honor and glory. We already know how the book of Revelation concludes!

First...A Look Back

In the letters to the churches, each church has received a different commendation and reprimand. The church at Ephesus was loyal to their faith and sound doctrine, yet they lacked love. Smyrna, the poor persecuted church, who was tried and found faithful in all her ways, received no reprimand. The church at Pergamos passionately stood for the name of Christ but lacked the same moral passion and some compromised in their faith. They were not practicing what they professed.

The fourth letter, which was written to the church at Thyatira, commended the people for their works, love, service, faith, and patience (v. 19). From the outside, Thyatira's church looked like a very vibrant, active, healthy church; however, the health of a church or a believer is never what it seems like to the world looking in. Christ alone sees and judges the heart's intent as displayed in the opening description of Christ being the One "who has eyes like a flame of fire, and His feet like fine brass." Christ's fiery eyes penetrate and judge the hearts of men.

This church had what Ephesus seemed to lack—a love for others, and Christ had some serious reprimands for the believers of Thyatira. He condemned them for allowing false teachers to seduce His people into committing sexual immorality and idolatry. Whereas some of the church people at Pergamos needed to repent of sins and worldliness, at Thyatira, these issues became even more blatant as the church itself and its teachers not only tolerated but also signed off on and taught error contrary to the Word of God. Does what was happening in this church sound at all descriptive of our current society?

In calling this teacher *Jezebel*, Jesus likely was alluding to the fact that this teacher was much like ueen Jezebel, who once reigned with her husband, Ahab, over Israel (I Kings 16:31-32; 18:13-46; 19:1-3; 21:1-16; II Kings 9). I Kings records some of Jezebel's actions that reveal similarities between the two women. She portrayed herself as someone very spiritual yet led God's people to worship Baal and then turn to idolatry and indulge in sexual immorality. God used his prophet Elijah to overcome this idol worship by challenging their belief system and setting the power of their gods in opposition against the one true God. Elijah did win against the false prophets through relying on God. II Kings 9 reveals the subsequent fate of Jezebel as she was thrown from the palace window, trampled to death and eaten by dogs. God's heart can be seen through this account, as well as how seriously He takes sin. As believers who are to have a heart for the things of God, Elijah vs. Jezebel should leave us with a question to ponder: Do I take sin as seriously as God?

Two Paths: One leads to Life, One to Death

The account of Thyatira addresses two groups: those who were corrupt and the remnant who remained faithful. This letter tells the fate of those who were corrupt and unwilling to repent of their false beliefs and teachings (as Christ would bring judgment against them). Though Christ judged, we must never forget how gracious and loving our God is and how His heart's desire was for them to repent. God desires that none should perish but that all would turn to Christ and be saved (2 Peter 3:9) He gave these false teachers time to repent, but they would not.

The warning for us today is also to understand the heart of Christ regarding sin. God hates sin, and Romans 6:11 instructs us to reckon ourselves dead to sin. In understanding the consequences sin brought to the world and continues to bring, we should no longer desire to walk as those in darkness but as children of light (Ephesians 5:6-11). Throughout the Scripture, Christ is clear about our call to walk by the Spirit and not to tolerate sin any more than Christ does.

TOO MANY believers today are seemingly embracing sin as Thyatira did and signing off on egregious sin, even indoctrinating it into the church. This must not be! The call of the believer is no longer to conform to the ways of the world but to present themselves a living sacrifice, holy and acceptable to God, which is the only reasonable response to what Christ did.

As believers, we are called to be transformed through the renewing of our minds to prove what is that good and acceptable will of our Heavenly Father (Romans 12:1-2). We are called to be holy as He is holy! AS HE IS HOLY (1 Peter 1:16)! These calls for transformation leave no room for sin in our lives. Saying we must not let sin abound so that grace may abound misses the point. The point is that sin did abound, but fortunately, grace abounded more on the cross! Yet we, as the dearly beloved of Christ, are to no longer walk as those who are perishing. What sense does it make for a child of God to walk as those to whom the wrath of God will be poured out?

We were delivered from that fate and are no longer slaves of sin but free to live for Christ. Titus clarifies this altogether for us in stating in chapter 2:11-14, which says,

> For the grace of God that brings salvation has appeared to all men, teaching us that, denying ungodliness and worldly lusts, we should live soberly, righteously, and godly in the present age, looking for the blessed hope and glorious appearing of our great God and Savior Jesus Christ, who gave Himself for us, that He might redeem us from every lawless deed and purify for Himself *His* own special people, zealous for good works.

The Story of Demas

Three Scriptures introduce the Bible character named Demas, who is first mentioned in Colossians 4:10-14, along with at least eight other believers with Paul in Rome where he is a prisoner. In Philemon, Demas is named as being with Paul as a fellow laborer in the ministry. Approximately four to five years after the first mention of Demas in

Colossians, Paul, who was imprisoned and waiting to be martyred near the end of his life, writes in II Timothy 4:10, "Demas has forsaken me, having loved this present world, and has departed for Thessalonica."

We are not told what Demas loved in the world that drew him away from serving Christ. Bible teacher, Gordon Franz, says the following concerning Demas:

> This world system has only three allurements to draw the believer away from his or her love for the Lord. First, there is the lust of the flesh, second, the lust of the eyes, and finally, the pride of life. The first, the lust of the flesh, has to do with the gratification of the flesh (what makes me feel good physically). Included within this allurement would be sexual sins, gluttony, drug use, and drunkenness. The second category is the lust of the eyes (what possessions I want to make me happy). The final category is pride of life (what I want to be... [power/position]). This is the arrogance that one has when they boast about themselves, their accomplishments, or their possessions. Whatever Demas' love for the world was, it fell into at least one of these three categories[15].

Scripture warns [as previously covered] that the Enemy walks around like a roaring lion seeking whom he may devour and that his plan is to kill steal and destroy, but for Christians to be strong in the Lord and in the power of His might, they must put on the full armor of God so that they can stand against evil. The Enemy can tempt, but we cannot blame him. Matthew 15:19 says, "For out of the heart proceed

---

[15] Franz, G. (2009). Life and Land » Blog Archive » DEMAS: Lover of this Present World. [online] Lifeandland.org. Available at: https://www.lifeandland.org/2009/03/demas-lover-of-this-present-world/

evil thoughts, murders, adulteries, fornication, thefts, false witness, blasphemies." When those at Thyatira stand before God, they will not be able to blame anyone else for their actions, and neither will we. The sins of this church speak directly to our great need to allow Christ to come into our lives and change our hearts—to give us a new heart.

What the Bible does not say about Demas is how his life ended. Perhaps he eventually turned back, but what it seems is that he abandoned his faith for the world. If this were the case, I would tend to believe he was never truly saved. How sad a turn of events when considering his end—if he never did repent and turn back to Christ.

A Different Story: The Faithful at Thyatira, Mark, You?

From those at Thyatira and Demas, we need to learn to hold a broader view of life than to live only to fulfill the immediate gratifications of the flesh over serving Christ. We should have an eternal outlook and understanding of what is truly important. We must remember how dependent we are on Christ to remain faithful, and one day, we will all be judged. Therefore, we must be determined to persevere in the faith.

As for Demas, how sad to have been a servant of God who seemed to have begun so strong only to turn from the truth. His example is a warning for us to make sure we do not depart from the living God and from the only source of salvation—Christ. What I find interesting is the other name Paul mentioned after stating Demas had abandoned him in 2 Timothy 4:11—Mark. Whereas Demas seemed to start strong and ended weak in his faith, Mark started weak but kept his focus on Christ and grew strong in his faith. You could say, he took seriously the call of Hebrews 12 to cast off every weight and the sin that so easily entangles us and to keep our eyes on Christ the Author and Finisher of our faith.

Of course, some of those at Thyatira remained pure, and Christ encouraged them to hold on and to overcome. What about you? How will your story end? Christ warns those of Thyatira to repent. In Revelation 2:29, He earnestly pleaded with them and any others as such to understand and turn to Him to be saved while they can as he declares, "He who has an ear let him hear what the Spirit says to the churches!" That sentiment is repeated throughout the letters.

We must heed the words and warnings of Christ. As our Savior, Christ died because of sin, and God hates sin. True, when we are genuinely in Christ, God looks at us and does not see our sin (past, present, or future) and who of us can say we are without sin. The fact that God does not see our sins does not mean we are not to hate or grieve over our sin or have a repentant heart. NO! In Christ, we have been given a new heart, and with this new heart, we desire to live differently. This new heart views sin just like God, and though we fall, when we are in Christ we repent, get back up and are *never* okay with the sin that caused our Savior to go to the cross.

Though the world and even the churches around us may seem to embrace sin or at the very least appear to take it lightly, the call for the true believer is to *overcome*. The true believer is to overcome and keep the works of Christ alive in his life. We, as believers, must be about the work of Christ. True, we are saved by grace; being good or sinless in ourselves did not save us—only Christ's work on the cross alone saved us. Our good works after being saved do not keep us saved. Only by grace through trusting in Christ are we saved, yet we must not take sin lightly and cheapen the grace and sacrifice of Christ. We must redeem the time while we have the opportunity for the days indeed are evil (Ephesians 5:16). We must hold tightly to our faith in Christ and raise a standard against evil because God deserves to be honored. In merely hating sin and being obedient, we love Him in return for His first loving us.

Praise be to Christ the only hope for salvation. "For there is no other name under heaven given to mankind by which we must be saved" (Acts 4:12b). Thanks be to the One worthy of all honor glory and praise—Christ alone.

Seven Letters Study Guide
Chapter 4 — *The Church at Thyatira*

1. For what did Christ commend the church (if anything)? The commendations should encourage us to acquire these attributes desired in the Christian's life.

2. For what did Christ rebuke the church for (if anything)? Christ's rebuke should cause us to reflect and examine our own life against the rebuke. Do we need change?

    B. What was the warning or what could happen as a result of the troubled area not being addressed and mended?

3. Do you see any of the areas covered that need corrected as being problematic in the modern church? If so, what corrective action needs to be taken?

4. What additional thoughts came to mind when reviewing this letter? What else could have been highlighted or could we learn from the church of Thyatira?

5

Sardis—
The Dead Church

And to the angel of the church in Sardis write, "These things says He who has the seven Spirits of God and the seven stars: "I know your works, that you have a name that you are alive, but you are dead. Be watchful, and strengthen the things which remain, that are ready to die, for I have not found your works perfect before God. Remember therefore how you have received and heard; hold fast and repent. Therefore if you will not watch, I will come upon you as a thief, and you will not know what hour I will come upon you. You have a few names even in Sardis who have not defiled their garments; and they shall walk with Me in white, for they are worthy. He who overcomes shall be clothed in white garments, and I will not blot out his name from the Book of Life; but I will confess his name before My Father and before His angels. He who has an ear, let him hear what the Spirit says to the churches."

(Revelation 3:1-6)

5

Sardis—The Dead Church

(Revelation 3:1-6)

The message to the church at Sardis is rather simple, yet dreadful: you are dead. They had a name for themselves, yet when Christ surveyed them spiritually, He declared there was no life. While *dead* was descriptive of the church as a whole, He does instruct a remnant that remains to "Be watchful, and strengthen the things which remain, that are ready to die…" (v. 2a). *"Ready to die"* hints at the fact that in due time, if they do not act upon the command, even the remnant of those who are saved will become nonexistent.

After mentioning the things that remain needing strengthened, verse 2 concludes that He has not found their "works perfect before God." Apparently, this remnant was indifferent to the shortcoming of this church. The remnant was presently doing nothing to change the situation. Christ's call to this church is to remember what they had received and heard and to hold fast to these truths and repent. They needed to remember the faith upon which the church had been founded and return to it.

Take Action!

In short, the remnant needed to take action. The church, with the encouragement of the remnant, needed to return to having an active living faith. To do this, they needed to do the following:

- Not let the truth slip away from their midst
- Repent or change their way of thinking to what God declared to be the truth
- Live in the reality of this gospel
- Seek the things of God over the things of the world

Evidently, the people attending the church at Sardis were not attending out of pure love for Christ. Since most of them were not saved, they would have paid more attention to their worldly cares over the things of Christ. Perhaps they thought that the god they had created for themselves could give them more of the world. Unfortunately, many people today have this same problem. Perhaps it was all just the social aspect of church that brought many of them together. Whatever the reason most of them gathered at church, salvation wasn't involved.

We often hear of lukewarm churches as plaguing our current society. The main difference between the lukewarm church and the dead church is that of the former Christ does not speak of any being saved—only lukewarm. While Christ declares Sardis dead as a church, He mentions a remnant. While both descriptions have a strong application to modern churches, Sardis may be more comparative of many churches rather than their being lukewarm.

Christ Alone...

How many churches today seem to be alive, yet what they proclaim as the gospel falls short of the true gospel? The teachings do not clearly portray the depravity of mankind, the magnitude of mankind's sin condition and the only way to salvation – Christ.

The message not being articulated distinctly from many pulpits is the need for all to understand because of sin, the wrath of God is poured out on mankind. Who, if dying without receiving salvation are destined to pay the penalty of their sin eternally in a sinner's hell. Of their own, no man [or woman] can do anything to change this. A Holy God had to judge sin and He judged the wages of sin as death. Fortunately, God is not only Holy but loving and sent His only begotten Son into the world to die for sinners – to become a substitution sacrifice in their place. Yes that is right He is so Holy He had to judge sin but He is also so loving, knowing we could not save ourselves, He sent His Son to die in our place.

It is by His grace in being willing to die on the cross that we can be saved as we trust in Him [Christ] as our Savior. As we put our trust in Christ, God will account His death as the price being paid for our sins and we are saved. What a gift!

We must understand Christ is the only way to salvation! The death of Christ was the only death worthy to pay the penalty for sin and to restore our right standing with God. There is no other way leading to salvation only faith in Christ. And, it is important (a matter of life or death) that we get this right!

Another area where Preachers and pastors also often fail is by adding to the gospel. As mentioned, the only way to be saved is by grace - in trusting on the finished *work of Christ* on the cross alone - and not of any works man can add. While many either do not emphasize or proclaim the need for the blood atonement, as discussed previously, others add additional requirements to being saved, such as Christ plus baptism or Christ plus communion.

Adding these requirements is similar to what Paul strongly warned against in Galatians when some were teaching Christ plus circumcision. No matter what other requirements are added to being saved through grace by faith, a new gospel is created, which Paul declared to the churches in Galatia as being no gospel at all. Those who put their faith in such nonsense are accursed (Galatians 1:9).

I once spoke with a lady who proudly told me about the church she had been attending for five years. By her account, the church had thousands of members and had much happening. After listening to her regaling her church, I asked her what they taught about being saved.

She responded, "I don't know for sure. You would have to ask one of the pastors."

How this vague answer saddened my heart. I cannot fathom someone's attending a church for five years and being unable to articulate the gospel. The church must do infinitely better than this report!

While I could not tell you with certainty that this church aligned with the teaching on the church at Sardis, what I do know is that making disciples, which starts with the gospel being proclaimed, is where the church is to place its focus.

Live Like You Could Be in Christ's Presence at Any Moment...

We need to heed the words and warnings of Christ and keep the gospel central in our lives and in our churches. We must be watchful and not forget what saves us, for one day without warning, any of us could be in the presence of Christ. At this point, the spiritually dead would no longer have any hope for redemption; only those who remained in the faith (have not defiled their garments) would be safe (v. 4).

The promise to those who overcome is that they would walk with Him and that He would not blot their name from the Book of Life (v. 5). This verse is often misused by those who believe a saved person can lose his salvation; however, the verse simply does not say this. We must be careful not to add what is not there to Scriptures. This verse is merely a promise to the faithful that Christ will not remove their names from the Book of Life and they can be assured of their salvation. To add more to the Scripture is to add what it does not clearly say or point to. This verse is instead a figure of speech that affirms the positive results from those who overcome[16]. Christ also speaks of those who overcome that He will confess their names before His Father and the angels. He will declare that they are His. What a great promise and encouragement!

The Need to Seek God with Their Whole Heart!

If you survey the Scripture for the times when the church or God's people strayed from Him, the call to the remnant was always to turn to Him, repent, and seek Him. Deuteronomy chapter 4 tells about a time that, after entering the Promised Land, the people turned from God to their idols and, as a result, suffered correction. The instructions at that time were for the remnant to seek God with their whole heart and soul and, in doing so, God would remember His covenant and bring new life and blessings to them (Deuteronomy 4:29-31). The word *seek* used in Deuteronomy 4 is more than simply looking for Him; it is a passionate endeavor to follow after God.

Similarly, this passionate endeavor to find God is what He wants of the church at Sardis—to remember the faith they were founded on and to repent. In doing so, they would be passionately pursuing Him so new life could be born into their dying church. The call was for the remnant to fan the flames of revival in their midst, relying wholly on God. Likewise, the call for every believer is to passionately seek God

---

[16]MacArthur, J. (1992). Sardis: The Dead Church. [online] Grace to You. Available at: https://www.gty.org/library/sermons-library/66-11/sardis-the-dead-church

continually, so our lives and churches never resemble the dead church at Sardis.

As Christ Himself so passionately addressed in this letter to the church at Sardis, eternal life and death are at stake. "He who has an ear, let him hear what the Spirit says to the churches."

Seven Letters Study Guide
Chapter 5 — *The Church of Sardis*

1. For what did Christ commend the church (if anything)? The commendations should encourage us to acquire these attributes desired in the Christian's life.

2. For what did Christ rebuke the church (if anything)? Christ's rebuke should cause us to reflect and examine our own life against the rebuke. Do we need change?

    B. What was the warning or what could happen as a result of the troubled area not being addressed and mended?

3. Do you see any of the areas covered that need corrected as being problematic in the modern church? If so, what corrective action needs to be taken?

4. What additional thoughts came to mind when reviewing this letter? What else could have been highlighted or could we learn from the church at Sardis?

6

Philadelphia—
The Faithful Church

"And to the angel of the church in Philadelphia write, "These things says He who is holy, He who is true, "He who has the key of David, He who opens and no one shuts, and shuts and no one opens. I know your works. See, I have set before you an open door, and no one can shut it; for you have a little strength, have kept My word, and have not denied My name. Indeed I will make those of the synagogue of Satan, who say they are Jews and are not, but lie—indeed I will make them come and worship before your feet, and to know that I have loved you. Because you have kept My command to persevere, I also will keep you from the hour of trial which shall come upon the whole world, to test those who dwell on the earth. Behold, I am coming quickly! Hold fast what you have, that no one may take your crown. He who overcomes, I will make him a pillar in the temple of My God, and he shall go out no more. I will write on him the name of My God and the name of the city of My God, the New Jerusalem, which comes down out of heaven from My God. And I will write on him My new name. He who has an ear, let him hear what the Spirit says to the churches."

(Revelation 3:7-13)

6

Philadelphia— The Faithful Church

(Revelation 3:7-13)

"Well done, thy good and faithful servant" are words that every believer hopes to hear Jesus declare over his life after all is said and done. Believers who will receive this commendation are those who attended the church in Philadelphia. Jesus had no criticism of this church—only commendation. The church at Philadelphia is a picture of those that are faithful.

The opening address to the church reveals the features of this church. Out of His omniscient (all-knowing) character, Christ sees their works/deeds—as He has seen the works of the other churches. Jesus names three characteristics of this church in regard to their faithfulness:

- The open door that was before them
- Their enduring despite having little strength
- They kept His Word while not denying His name

I Have Set Before You an Open Door...

The first characteristic of this church is that Jesus has set an open door in front of them. Pastor David Guzik states that an open door often speaks of evangelistic opportunity (1 Corinthians 16:9, 2 Corinthians 2:12, and Colossians 4:3)[17]. Jesus has told them He opened the door of evangelistic opportunity for them, and they took advantage of the opportunity before them.

Of a certainty this open door speaks of their salvation and faith, but the fact that Jesus didn't rebuke them for their lack of love toward others as He did the Ephesians likely indicates that they also spread the gospel to others. Much can be told about people and their walk with the Lord by their motivation to reach out to others. Do they care if others are reached with the gospel message? Do they care about the things of Christ?

Christ cared enough to leave glory, live among sinful men who despised Him and, in the end, to offer up His own life on behalf of all mankind. What a price He paid to show how much He cared for the lost! How about us? Is the gospel and the salvation of others being saved important to us? Do we have a heart for the lost? Does our concern for the lost extend beyond a mere proclamation into taking action to see the gospel message is going forth?

Thou Hast Little Strength...

The first beatitude of Jesus' Sermon on the Mount states, "Blessed are the poor in spirit: for theirs is the kingdom of heaven" (Matthew 5:3). In their having *little strength*, those of the church at Philadelphia likely exemplified this verse. They knew they needed Christ in their life, and

---

[17] Guzik, D. "Study Guide for Revelation 3 by David Guzik." Blue Letter Bible. Last Modified 21 Feb, 2017. https://www.blueletter-bible.org/Comm/guzik_david/StudyGuide2017-Rev/Rev-3.cfm

as such, they relied on God. The church was humbled before God and sought after Him.

Luke 7:36-50 validates an example of this type of humble heart when Jesus was invited to eat at the house of Simon, a Pharisee. A woman described as a sinner heard Jesus would be there and went to meet Him. During the dinner, she brought an alabaster box of ointment and she wept at Jesus' feet, she washed them with her tears and anointed them. No doubt she understood her need for Christ. Her loving, submissive encounter with Jesus was much different than that of Simon, whose pharisaical heart immediately cast judgment on the woman's cherishing of Jesus. He thought, "This man, if he were a prophet, would have known who and want manner of woman this is that toucheth him: for she is a sinner" (Luke 7:39b).

Knowing Simon's judgmental thoughts, Jesus told a story of two debtors whose debt was discharged by their master. The debtor who was forgiven more would love the master more. The woman pictured the debtor between her and Simon of the one who was forgiven of more debt. The woman who washed Jesus' feet with her tears was, in fact, the only one forgiven for she realized her sin and the need for forgiveness. This forgiveness of sin was the reason for her great outpouring of love for Christ while Simon showed Christ no honor at the dinner. He too should have been at the feet of Jesus, asking for mercy from a Master who would have freely forgiven the debt of his sin.

We must ask ourselves the following questions:

- Have I had an encounter with Jesus like this woman?

- Have I ever gone beyond the pharisaical attitude of Simon the Pharisee?

- Have I accepted Jesus (as the Pharisee did into his home), yet not realized how spiritually poor I am?

- Have I truly repented and received the gift of salvation that belongs only to Christ to give?

If we have put our faith in Christ, what should the effect be? We can see this in how Jesus responds to the woman. Jesus first forgives her sin (v. 48), then He instructs her to go in peace for her faith in Him has saved her (v. 50). This woman now had a new life, and she left the presence of Jesus a different person than when she came to that dinner!

Has Kept My Word, and Hast Not Denied My Name...

We also see that the church at Philadelphia was faithful; they kept His word.

> The idea behind the phrase, *have not denied My name,* is not only that they expressed their allegiance to Jesus, but they lived in a way that was faithful to the name and character of Jesus (Guzik)[18].

Jesus commends the church at Philadelphia for not *denying* His name. True, "not denying His name" means that if asked or challenged, the person would not deny Jesus as Lord and Savior. However, the tense of the Greek word *arneomai (ar-ne'-o-mi)* which is used for "deny," has a much deeper meaning. The original Greek not only illustrates denying someone else but also one's own self—to act entirely unlike himself[19]. One of the Ten Commandments is not to take the name of

---

[18] Ibid.
[19] "G720 - arneomai - Strong's Greek Lexicon (NKJV)." Blue Letter Bible. Accessed 31 Aug, 2019. https://www.blueletterbible.org//lang/lexicon/lexicon.cfm?Strongs=G720&t=NKJV

the Lord God in vain (Exodus 20:7). This verse is most often considered applicable to using God's name inappropriately or accompanied with a swear word, but I believe the meaning can be much more profound and broader. I believe we can take the name of the Lord in vain when we accept the name *child of God*, without any change in our life. *Vain* or *vanity* from the Hebrew *shav'* means "emptiness or falsehood." You could even say "meaningless." So, if I call myself a Christian or a believer, but my life does not conform to God's ways, my so-called Christianity is meaningless and taking His name in vain. *Many profess to be Christians, but the Christian character they display does not support this profession.* Some in the church at Pergamos also had this problem; the faith they professed wasn't always the faith they practiced.

When Christians deny the name of Christ, they forsake or give up the way of life intended for them to live. After all, we either live by the Spirit or the flesh.

2 Timothy 3 lists the traits of those who confess to have a faith contrasted against those who have true faith in Christ. Verses two through five list the characteristics of those teachers [and the like] who are genuinely not of the faith: "lovers of self, lovers of money, boasters, proud, blasphemers, disobedient to parents, unthankful, unholy, unloving, unforgiving, slanderers, without self-control, brutal, despisers of good, traitors, headstrong, haughty, lovers of pleasure rather than lovers of God, having a form of godliness, but denying its power." In other words, they do not have a repentant heart or care to exercise themselves toward godliness. They are not changed by the Word of God nor led by the Spirit.

Those of the faith who are truly saved and filled with the Spirit are changed forever as Paul explains later in 2 Timothy 3 when he lists their traits: "But you have carefully followed my doctrine, manner of life, purpose, faith, longsuffering, love, perseverance" (v. 10). In other words, their faith had changed them. Not only did they profess they were a disciple of Christ but were indeed a disciple in practice. Those who had accepted the saving grace of Jesus believed verses 16 and 17: "All scripture is given by inspiration of God, and is profitable for doctrine, for reproof, for correction, for instruction in righteousness, that the man of God may be complete, thoroughly equipped for every good work." They desired to know Christ and to emulate His life.

What Say You?

How do you stack up against 2 Timothy chapter 3? To what are you committed in life? These Scriptures give direction for living—either we live by the flesh and its desires, or we live by the Word of God.

Romans 8:1 tells us we are not condemned in Christ, but being "set free" does not mean we should continue in sin. We are called to distinguish between what is holy and what is ordinary; we are not freed *to* sin but freed *from* sin!

We have often referenced the plight of the Israelites of the Old Testament after being freed from their lives of slavery in Egypt. The book of Exodus chronicles their plight. They spent 40 years in the wilderness, where nearly all of those initially freed would die. God had a Promised Land waiting for them, but their lack of faith prevented their taking that land of promise.

When the millions of people arrived at the Promised Land, twelve spies were dispatched to scout the land God had promised them. Of the twelve sent to scout the territory, only two of the twelve came back and displayed enough faith to enter. The other ten lacked confidence and voted to stay where they were, eventually dying in the wilderness, never receiving the gift of the Promised Land because of fear. "We are like grasshoppers to the enemies there," they argued even as the two faithful spies believed their God was bigger than the enemy ahead.

Yes, some battles would be fought in taking the Promised Land, but the battle was the Lord's. All God's people need was enough faith to go forward.

What do you need to have the confidence to go forward? You can keep going around that mountain in the wilderness until you die like the majority of Israelites who had been freed from Egypt did or you can walk in faith and be more than a conqueror. In Christ, you can walk in the victory He has already secured for you!

We have a choice to make. In Deuteronomy 10:12-21, Moses instructed the Israelites to fear the Lord and to walk in His ways. Joshua 24:14 and 15 shows that even after entering the Promised Land, the Israelites were still challenged to live in their old ways. Their call was simple: to keep their faith or look to God for their hope in every situation or challenge they faced in life. God wanted them to be sincere in their faith. We too are to be faithful to that upward calling. Will you rise to that challenge?

The church at Philadelphia took advantage of the evangelistic opportunity before them, they relied on God, and they kept His Word. Their choice to take advantage of the evangelistic opportunity does not sound very spectacular, does it? But it is! Their faith changed their lives, and their faith changed their eternal destiny!

One day every knee will bow humbly before Christ as the woman of Luke chapter 7 did, but for some, it will be too late. NOW is the time to accept Christ in faith. NOW is the time to see the open door. NOW is the time to rely on Christ. NOW is the time to be faithful. Choose NOW this day whom you will serve.

Act NOW and having received Christ as Savior, **HOLD FAST WHAT YOU HAVE!**

Seven Letters Study Guide
Chapter 6 — *The Church at Philadelphia*

1. For what did Christ commend the church (if anything)? The commendations should encourage us to acquire these attributes desired in the Christian's life.

2. For what did Christ rebuke the church (if anything)? Christ's rebuke should cause us to reflect and examine our own life against the rebuke. Do we need change?

    B. What was the warning or what could happen as a result of the troubled area not being addressed and mended?

3. Do you see any of the areas covered that need corrected as being problematic in the modern church? If so, what corrective action needs to be taken?

4. What additional thoughts came to mind when reviewing this letter? What else could have been highlighted or could we learn from the church of Philadelphia?

7

Laodicea—
The Lukewarm Church

"And to the angel of the church of the Laodiceans write, "These things says the Amen, the Faithful and True Witness, the Beginning of the creation of God: I know your works, that you are neither cold nor hot. I could wish you were cold or hot. So then, because you are lukewarm, and neither cold nor hot, I will vomit you out of My mouth. Because you say, "I am rich, have become wealthy, and have need of nothing"—and do not know that you are wretched, miserable, poor, blind, and naked— I counsel you to buy from Me gold refined in the fire, that you may be rich; and white garments, that you may be clothed, that the shame of your nakedness may not be revealed; and anoint your eyes with eye salve, that you may see. As many as I love, I rebuke and chasten. Therefore be zealous and repent. Behold, I stand at the door and knock. If anyone hears My voice and opens the door, I will come in to him and dine with him, and he with Me. To him who overcomes I will grant to sit with Me on My throne, as I also overcame and sat down with My Father on His throne. He who has an ear, let him hear what the Spirit says to the churches."

(Revelation 3:14-22)

7

Laodicea— The Lukewarm Church

(Revelation 3:14-22)

Some troubling issues have already been addressed in some of the previous letters, but I feel an extra heavy heart as I approach this last letter. Consider the plight of those who do not heed God's call— an eternity separated from God in a sinner's hell with no chance of reprieve. So, I fearfully and prayerfully address this last letter written to the church at Laodicea. I also believe it is of no coincidence that Christ places this letter last.

This letter portrays God's empathy as He implores those outside the safety of salvation that only He can offer to come to Him and freely receive His gift. The other letters also addressed the lost with the final plea included in them. And in considering this aspect, my heart was heavy, considering all those who will ignore the offer of salvation from Christ until it is too late.

I cannot help but think of the words of Matthew 23:37 that Jesus spoke as He approached Jerusalem and looked down upon the people:

> "O Jerusalem, Jerusalem, the one who kills the prophets and stones those who are sent to her! How often I wanted

to gather your children together, as a hen gathers her chicks under her wings, but you were not willing!"

He wanted so badly for the people to have the life He was offering. *If only they could see their great need and turn to Him [Christ] as Savior.* In Revelation 3:20, Jesus declares, "Behold, I stand at the door, and knock...." Then He promises those who will let Him come into their life that He will dine (enter into a relationship) with them. This relationship with Him will bring new life and hope for the future that affects the present. This hope stems from having peace with God Himself. So many ignore the call, leaving Him outside the door of their heart and never receiving what they so desperately need. Sadly, so many are like this. My prayer is for them to understand the message of this letter and turn to Christ before it is too late.

Letter from the Amen, the Faithful and True, the Beginning

Every letter to the churches in Revelation starts with a statement on the One from whom the message has come. The letter to the church of the Laodiceans is from "the Amen, the Faithful and True Witness, the Beginning of the creation of God." The description of each individualized introduction refers to the description of Jesus in Revelation 1. This narrative points to the True One, the beginning.

Of importance to note is the word *beginning*, which is the Greek word ***arche*** (ar-khay). In verse 14 the meaning for *beginning* is not "first in order," but "source or origin[20]." Jesus is the One from whom all creation originated, and as such, He is above all creation. This meaning is quite significant as it is a call for those to whom this letter applies to take these words very seriously. After all these words came from

---

[20] "G746 - archē - Strong's Greek Lexicon (NKJV)." Blue Letter Bible. Accessed 31 Aug, 2019. https://www.blueletterbible.org//lang/lexicon/lexicon.cfm?Strongs=G746&t=NKJV

the Creator God who not only spoke everything into existence but sustains all, and as the True One is the only One able and qualified to sit as judge over all! The "Amen, the Faithful and True Witness, the Beginning of the creation of God" should be revered and His words of wisdom should be taken seriously.

And what does He say of the church? He declares this group of believers is neither cold nor hot, but lukewarm (Revelation 3:16). To be lukewarm is the saddest of states for people who have heard His message and proclaim to know Him. Yet, from Christ's declaration, clearly they don't. They are unsaved, and as such, Jesus says that He will vomit them from His mouth in declaring His distaste of how carelessly and halfheartedly they approach Him and the gospel.

Rich and Have Need of Nothing

The attitude of this group bespeaks the fact they have become wealthy and have need of nothing. From the outside, they may look to be successful and blessed—both as a group and individually—yet Jesus said their true status was not so. They may have had worldly possessions, but spiritually, they were "wretched, miserable, poor, blind, and naked" (v. 17). In other words, they were unsaved and did not see their separation from God due to their sin and their great need for Him. They already thought they had enough of Him. They were in the same position as many false believers: "a form of godliness" (2 Timothy 3:5) but not a godliness that changes them along with their destiny. As Charles Spurgeon was once noted to say, "The grace that does not change my life will not save my soul."

Charles Spurgeon said the following of the "believers" at Laodicea:

> They are not so cold as to abandon their work, or to give up their meetings for prayer, or to reject the gospel [completely]. If they did, then they could be convinced of their

error and brought to repentance; but on the other hand are neither hot for the truth, not for conversions, nor hot for holiness, they are not fiery enough to burn the stubble of sin, nor zealous enough to make Satan angry, nor fervent enough to make a living sacrifice of themselves upon the altar of their God. They are neither cold nor hot[21]."

This paragraph describes the state of many who still call themselves Christians. Many even regularly attend church or religious events (albeit they would not care to miss them either), but they do not recognize their spiritual poverty and need to fall at the feet of Jesus and ask for His grace and mercy to save them. Only then will they have a genuine concern to see others become disciples so they too are spared God's judgment. However, in all manners of their faith, they are lukewarm. They will tell you they are believers and have a concern for others, but their actions and nonchalant attitude toward spiritual matters. They do not understand how spiritually bankrupt they are and in need of Christ.

As I wrote this final chapter, the rich young ruler Jesus spoke of in Matthew 19:16-22 was on my heart. The rich young ruler could not see how much he needed Jesus. He relied on his accomplishments, seeing himself as good and deserving of salvation from God, or that God would accept him because of his obedience and, in general, he was a good person. He tells Jesus he has kept the whole law in declaring his righteousness. When the rich man asks if he is missing any works to be saved, Jesus challenges him to sell everything he has and give it all to the poor. If indeed he kept the law perfectly, the rich young ruler would have had no problem selling all and giving to the poor out

---

[21] Spurgeon, C. (2013). 1176. An Earnest Warning Against Lukewarmness. [online] Answers in Genesis. Available at: https://answersingenesis.org/education/spurgeon-sermons/1176-an-earnest-warning-against-lukewarmness/

of love of neighbor. Instead, he went away sad at this request from Christ, as he was very wealthy.

What is disturbing is that he did not see how truly unrighteous he was from this encounter and then turn to Christ, trusting in Him alone. Indeed, how sad for him to have faced Jesus and not understanding, rejected what he truly needed. He was so spiritually poor, instead allowing his earthly accomplishments and wealth to take precedence over his spiritual poverty.

How about you? Have you come to an understanding of how bankrupt you truly are without Christ? Do you see how nothing of yourself can earn your salvation? Salvation comes only by trusting in what Christ has done to save us. Our obedience then flows from our relationship *with* God—not *to* Him. Many people need a critical understanding of this relationship.

The Counsel of the Lord

Verse 18 tells the Laodicean people what the Lord wants them to do. The heart of Christ is for them to be saved as He instructs them to buy from Him gold refined in the fire that they may be rich, white garments to be clothed in His righteousness, and salve to anoint their eyes in order to see. These instructions picture a call for them to see their actual state and to turn to Him to be saved. It is because of His great love for them that He is rebuking them. His desire for them is to be zealous for what He offers, repent, and be saved. He tells them that He is standing at the door of the church and at each of their hearts—if they will only allow Him, He can change their life and change their eternity. However, they must be willing to heed His words and take an honest look at their state and what it takes to receive salvation.

He who has an ear, let him hear what the Spirit says to the churches! Once more these words beckon the reader to take the proclamation of Christ seriously. Do not quickly dismiss the letter; instead, deeply consider the implications. Understand you can do nothing to save yourself and are born dead in your sins and trespasses. Understand that a righteous holy God who had to judge and condemn sin is also a loving, merciful God who died in our place. All we must do is trust in His sacrifice today and be saved. Trust in Christ—the only name given under heaven by which you must be saved.

Jesus did not give up on those at Laodicea. He stood at the door and knocked; He remained persistent then, and He still knocks today. He still beckons those who are unsaved to open their lives to Him and receive the gift of salvation. How unfortunate for those at Laodicea that were so close to the gospel yet so far from understanding and receiving it... and for all who do not take the time to seriously contemplate the gospel and their true state in light of a Holy God. Who never open the door and let Christ into their life.

The words of Jesus found of Matthew 11:28 is Christ's declaration yet today: "Come to Me, all you who labor and are heavy laden, and I **will** give you rest."

"He who has an ear, let him hear what the Spirit says to the churches."

Seven Letters Study Guide
Chapter 7 — *The Church of Laodicea*

1. For what did Christ commend the church (if anything)? The commendations should encourage us to acquire these attributes desired in the Christian's life.

2. For what did Christ rebuke the church (if anything)? Christ's rebuke should cause us to reflect and examine our own life against the rebuke. Do we need change?

    B. What was the warning or what could happen as a result of the troubled area not being addressed and mended?

3. Do you see any of the areas covered that need corrected as being problematic in the modern church? If so, what corrective action needs to be taken?

4. What additional thoughts came to mind when reviewing this letter? What else could have been highlighted or could we learn from the church of Laodicea?

Thank You!

Thank you for reading *Weighed in the Balances: How Would Christ Evaluate Your Faith?* It is my prayer this writing has both challenged and encouraged you.

If this book has blessed you, please remember to leave an online review. And, please check out these other titles *Prepare for War: Put on the Full Armor of God* and *You Think What: 21 Days to a More Positive Outlook on Life.*

In Christ,

Benjamin H. Woodcox